Contents

Introduction

House group organizers or co-ordinators always seem to be looking for new leaders to lead house groups. For this reason these notes have been written with the needs of the beginner in mind. They provide on-the-job leadership training for the novice and a good excuse for a refresher course for old hands!

Approach
Each session contains two types of material: notes for the leader, and a script. The notes suggest ways in which the leader can guide the group through each study, while the script provides the less confident group leader with a way of explaining the programme step by step.

The script can simply be read aloud to the group. However, the group as a whole will feel more at ease if the leader is able to give details and lead discussion in a more relaxed way, rather than

PEOPLE LIKE US

JOHN DAVIS & BOB MOFFETT

Scripture Union
130 City Road, London EC1V 2NJ

© 1989 John Davis and Bob Moffett

First published 1989 by Scripture Union
130 City Road, London EC1V 2NJ

ISBN 0 86201 563 4

British Library Cataloguing in Publication Data
Davis, John
    People like us.
    1. Bible. Characters
    I. Title II. Moffett, Bob
    220.9'2

    ISBN 0–86201–563–4

Illustrations: Taffy Davies

Typeset by Input Typesetting Ltd, London

Printed and bound in Great Britain by
Cox and Wyman Ltd, Reading

reading it 'straight' from the book. More confident leaders should use the script as a guide only.

Goals

1 Fellowship

The main purpose of this series of housegroup studies is to enable members of the larger church fellowship to get to know one another better. In a small group we can meet each other at a much deeper level than is possible in a large congregation. The role of the leader is to help facilitate this meeting. The times of informal 'coffee and chat' which form part of the group sessions along with the more structured times of discussion, are intended to contribute to the building of fellowship bonds.

It is important to grasp that *the group sessions are not intended simply to be times of stimulating discussion.* Rather, they should result in group members feeling they have discovered and revealed a little more about themselves and have begun to relate more deeply to others in the group.

2 Introduction to Bible study

This process of self-understanding and deepening relationships will be taken further as group members identify with the biblical characters in question and share as much or as little about their similarity with them as they feel able. For this reason the Bible studies are designed to be 'low key' rather than academic. By introducing Bible characters in this way group members will be able to identify with and learn from them. They will find it is an appetising and relevant way in to Bible study.

3 Practical action in church and neighbourhood
These groups should not end up as cosy corners for Christians to talk and chat! The result of all Bible study should eventually be practical action as we begin to understand more of how God wants us to live. Simple exercises are therefore suggested for the group at the end of each session, outlining ways in which the session's teaching can be applied in practical, down-to-earth ways.

4 Developing gifts of ministry and service
A gift- or ability-spotting exercise is woven into this series. Over the weeks group members are encouraged to discover more about their own gifts and those of other group members. The aim is to encourage group members to put those gifts into action in the work and ministry of the wider church fellowship. There is a suggestion at the end of the book for a special service in which those gifts can be offered to God's use.

Training
If this course is being followed by two or more housegroups in your church you may like to get together with an experienced group leader to go through some of the material in advance. The group leader's notes which follow can provide the basis for a training session. They give advice on how to lead a group along with information about this series and what it contains. This will be of value both to experienced leaders as well as those leading for the first time. It would be good to invite other housegroup leaders, potential or actual, to join you for the training session, even though they may be following different courses with their groups at present. The cartoons can be photo-

copied onto OHP acetates for use in the training session. There are also notes on leading a training session (pages 93–95) which you could give to the person who will be taking on this role.

After the groups have been running for two or three sessions it might be helpful to hold a 'follow-up' session for the group leaders. This will provide an opportunity to bring up problems or questions which can be worked through together. It also gives group leaders a wider view of what is happening in other groups; this can be both helpful and encouraging. For instance, it can be encouraging to know that you are not the only group leader with members who say nothing throughout the entire session, despite efforts to involve them!

This session will also give you the opportunity to go over the gift-and ability-spotting exercise with other leaders to clarify the mechanics of the exercise. If your church is planning a special service for the dedication of gifts and abilities at the end you may need to hold one last session with the other group leaders in order to discuss details of organization for the service.

Leader's notes

Initial contact with group members
Introduce yourself to each potential member before the first housegroup, inviting each one personally to come. Give them details of time and place and ask them to bring a Bible along. Assure them that meetings will end punctually, so that they can arrange babysitters, etc, with confidence.

The personal touch

Make a note of some general information about each person – where they live, if they are new to the church, what their interests are. This will help you to introduce them to the whole group on the first evening.

If you are meeting less frequently than once a week, group members may appreciate a personal reminder beforehand so that they do not forget to turn up!

Group size

Group size
A good size of group is one of eight to twelve members. If you have more than twelve, fewer people will be happy to speak in group discussions. Working with a base of twelve will give you an average attendance of about eight or ten, as not every member will come to each session.

Hosting the group
If you are leading the group it is best not to try to take on the job of host as well. Instead, sound out one of the potential group members to see if they would be willing to act as host and accommodate

the group at his or her house. You will need someone with a room large enough for eight to ten people.

Before the first meeting, call to see your host and familiarize yourself with the room to be used. Ask the host to make sure that the chairs are set out in a circle, or so that everyone can see everyone else. It is particularly important that you, as group leader, can be seen by the whole group. Make sure that the host is clear about the layout and is happy with any other details of the evening.

See that the group does not outstay its welcome at the host's home. Make sure the meeting ends at a reasonable hour as the host may need to tidy up before retiring to bed. So be firm for his or her sake and see that the group leaves by the agreed time. If necessary, encourage the group to leave by saying something like, 'Well, I think it's time we were all going, so that our host can get to bed! Thank you . . . for your hospitality.'

A place where everyone can see you

Aims of the group leader

1 To help people get to know one another and develop friendships.

2 To promote discussion among the group. Simply teaching or preaching to the group will suppress discussion and prevent group members from making their own discoveries about themselves, each other, and the Bible character.

3 To encourage individual participation in group action exercises. These will help apply the subject under discussion to real-life situations.

4 To help group members discover and attempt to use their various gifts and abilities.

Preparation

Read the material through at least two or three times so that you are familiar with it, and prepare group exercises ahead of time. Introductory information is set out at the beginning of each session. Notes for the group leader are always set out in small, bold type.

Where material is to be presented verbally to the

Prepare well in advance of the meeting

group a suggested way of doing so is given in 'script' form, set in the larger typeface. It is not recommended that you use this as a total script which you read from beginning to end. It is simply intended as a guide to the shape and content of the various parts of the session. Should you lose your place, however, or become uncertain about what comes next, you could read the 'script' to introduce the next item.

Welcome

The welcome time forms a valuable part of the fellowship process, as does the coffee and chat at the end of the session. Giving your group time to talk and chat among themselves when they arrive not only provides a chance to get to know one another it also helps to create an informal atmosphere for the rest of the session. As the weeks go by it is important to watch that this period does not become longer and longer, thereby taking up a disproportionate amount of time. Ultimately you must be the final judge of how much time to spend on this from week to week.

Some people find it difficult to make the first move to introduce themselves. There may be group members who will need your help. So be on the lookout for members who sit in the same seat each week and only talk to those nearest to them. During the coffee and chat time at the end of the meeting, bring a different group member over to meet them, especially if you discover they have something in common.

Introductions

Set out below is a good way of making introductions when the group first meets. There is also an example of how it sounds in practice.

A little personal information to introduce new members

Introduce yourself first, and then introduce each member of the group. Do this by taking one person at a time and giving the others a little bit of personal information about him or her. Complete your introduction of each person by asking if you have got your facts right and by asking what name he or she would like to be known by in the group.

It may go a little like this:

'Let me take a moment at this point to introduce everybody. Maybe it's best if I begin with myself. My name is Valerie Martin. I'm a housewife and I have two girls, Karen aged seven and Gemma aged nine. I have a husband called John who's the manager of a TV rental shop. And, by the way, please call me Val rather than Valerie. As a girl, if my mother ever called me 'Valerie' I knew I was in trouble, because she normally called me Val. So if you call me Valerie I will think I am in trouble!

On my left is Margaret Browning. She is a retired lady who has two grown-up children. Both of them are married and live quite a way away. She has been a widow since the last war, so now lives on her own in Pimlico Street. Before retiring she worked for the Post Office for twenty-five years, I think, or have I got my facts wrong there? . . . Thanks. What name would you like to be known by here, Mags, Maggie, Margaret or something else?'

There is a good reason for introducing the group in this way: many people feel daunted and intimidated if they are asked to introduce themselves to a totally unfamiliar group of people. By doing it the way recommended here, each group member is invited to break the 'sound barrier' by correcting your introductory information about them, if they wish to, and by saying what name they would like to be known by in the group. If group members are put on the spot and asked to talk about themselves at this stage it can lead to an uneasiness which could affect the rest of the sessions. Some members may be worried that you will 'drop' on them to do or say other things in the future. There is a high risk that they might just opt out of the group now, rather than face the possibility of this happening.

Use of the Bible

Read the passage yourself, especially for the opening week or two. If you ask others to read, do so well in advance, giving them the chance to say no! If they *do* say no, do not try to talk them into changing their minds!
- Do not ask people to read aloud, one after the other, round the group.
- Do not ask people to read on the spot.

Reading around the group = panic!

There are good reasons for these statements:

1 Reading aloud can be very threatening for a none-too-confident reader, and can cause him to drop out of the group.

2 Not everyone likes reading aloud in public; it can be a very nerve-racking experience for some, especially if asked to read without warning.

3 The Bible has many difficult 'theological' words and unpronounceable names in it that can cause embarrassment to adults if they stumble over them.

4 Some people may have personal reasons, perhaps physical difficulties, for not wanting to read. If they are asked to read they may feel obliged to make these reasons public in order to excuse themselves, and feel embarrassed as a result.

5 Poor readers feel they are made to look inferior by the fact that others can read better than them.

Encourage individuals to bring their Bibles to the sessions, so that they can follow as the passage is read. Give plenty of time for people to find the passage. It helps if everyone has the same version, as this will enable you to give the page number. No one should feel embarrassed at having to look up a book in the 'contents' page at the front of their Bible. If your group are not familiar with the Bible it may be helpful to find the passage by looking together at the contents page.

Why not?
The 'Why Not?' part of each session is the easiest one to drop but probably the most useful way of helping individuals to get to know one another and to think through the issue under discussion.

Every group is made up of individuals who come with 'full' minds – the children's latest problem; the argument with their husband just before leaving; the mother who is ill or the neighbour across the road who suddenly seems very 'friendly' for no particular reason.

'Why not?' helps the group to set aside those worries for a while so that they can relate to each other on more or less the same wavelength, and concentrate together as a group.

'Why not?' needs the leader's enthusiasm. If you are half-hearted then it will become a pointless exercise and the 'core' teaching will suffer too.

'Why not?' helps the individual and the group to keep in mind the personal implications rather than the abstract theories which are usually more comfortable!

'Why not?', like the rest of the material, requires preparation. Failure to know your material will ALWAYS show.

'Why not?' is a useful tool and an integral part of this material. However, you must assess how suitable each is for your group. If you feel the group will not respond well to a particular idea, then leave it out.

Discussion
Here are some hints on leading and prompting discussion.

1 Do not be afraid of silence. In a group setting a few seconds can seem like a very long time! It is tempting to break it to help things along, but a time of reflective silence gives people time to think and pluck up courage to make a contribution.

2 Do not talk too much. If you do, you will get in the way of other people and prevent them from joining in. You will end up with a solo performance instead of a discussion.

3 Beware of being a preacher or a teacher – a point closely related to the last. The moment this happens the group becomes a class or a silent congregation; discussion and sharing become strained and the freedom on the part of group members to take part becomes restricted.

4 Avoid over-reacting to silent members of the group. You may well find you have group members who rarely if ever say anything. They may be perfectly content to sit and listen to others making their contributions to the discussion. Do not set yourself the objective of getting them to say something at each session. This will put silent members under undue pressure and give you unnecessary feelings of failure when you do not achieve your objective!

On the other hand, do not ignore them, making

Don't be afraid of silence

no attempt to involve them in the discussion. Once they have settled into the group you could ask, at an appropriate moment, if they have any thoughts on the subject under discussion. Or you could ask if they agree or disagree with a particular view that has just been expressed. If they give only a one- or two-word answer you could sensitively ask them why they take that view.

If on other occasions you see that they are attempting to join in, but their contribution gets crowded out by other group members, go back to them as soon as possible and ask them what it was that they were about to say.

5 Try to keep the group moving through the questions. You do not want to get bogged down on just one or two questions. However, you probably will not have time to attempt *all* the questions, so watch the clock and be selective. It is very important to allow a reasonable amount of time for the report-back and action sections. If necessary, cut back on the questions to ensure that report back and action sections are covered.

Under some questions you will find sub-questions which you can use to extend the discussion of a particular subject. See, for example, question 3 on page 61 and question 2 on page 82.

6 If the group has difficulty answering a particular question avoid answering it for them. Prompt them in some way first or put the question another way round before giving them the answer. If you do not do this the object of group discussion will be eroded. In some of the more difficult questions, however, suggestions to help you are given in the form of leader's notes. They are *not* to be regarded as definitive answers, as this will be sure to kill all genuine discussion. Use them as a guide for the general direction of the discussion.

Coping with an over-talkative member
What can you do if one member dominates the discussions? Here are some suggestions. As a first step, ask him or her not to answer the next question so that others can share in the discussion. Alternatively, ask for comments from those who have not taken much part in the discussion so far.

How to cope with an over-talkative member

If each of these strategies fails have a discreet word with the person concerned *on his own*. You could try one of the following approaches:

1 The sensitive approach: 'Jim, I seem to be cutting you off an awful lot in the group meetings lately. I hope you aren't offended? You obviously enjoy taking part but so do others and I have to give them a chance too. Could you help me by holding back a bit in the discussion? Or when I cut you short it will look as though I am singling you out each week.'

2 A cry-for-help approach: 'Jim, could I ask for your help in the housegroup? I am having difficulty in seeing fair play in the discussion time; not everyone gets a chance to join in, especially some of the more silent members. Would you give me a little help by holding back a bit on your contributions for a while so that the discussion gets shared around a bit more? That will give me a chance to involve some of those who are slower to join in.'

3 The direct approach: 'Jim, please don't take any offence at this but could you hold back in the discussion at the housegroup? At the moment there is a real danger of the discussion being dominated by your enthusiasm to join in, and my job as group leader is to avoid that by involving as many people as I can.'

Action and report back
These sections are designed to take your group beyond the point of discussion. They encourage

the group to think of practical steps that can be taken in the light of the topic under discussion. The group agrees its own form of action, then reports back at the next session on how things have gone with their attempts to implement their ideas. Usually, as a group begins to gel, its members become willing to have a go at doing something if others in the group are making a similar effort. Less confident members are often happy to try something with the help of another group member which they would not be prepared to do on their own.

The idea is that the *group* takes up the ideas it feels happy with, and implements them. Group leaders are part of the group and it is hoped they will join in this action! But it is not the group leader's task to carry out the action on behalf of the group. It is group action which is required. It may be helpful to look at one or two examples at this point, so take a look at the 'Action' section on pages 30–31 and the 'Report back' on page 34.

Gift and ability-spotting exercise
As part of the Action and Report-back sections a gift and abilities exercise has been built in. This can develop into a positive and productive exercise if it is tackled confidently. The idea is to get group members to list the gifts and abilities which they feel others in the group possess, along with the gifts and abilities they feel they possess themselves. These are listed on large stones or stone-shaped pieces of coloured card a little larger than the size of a hand. They can, if you wish be shaped like a house brick.

The exercise is based on the idea of 'living stones' in 1 Peter 2:4–5 and on the importance of using what spiritual gifts God has given to each of us in the life of his church (1 Peter 4: 10–11). The stones or cardboard cut-outs become the material on which individual lists of group members' gifts and abilities are set out. They can also be used in the context of a service for an act of dedication (see pages 92–93).

Prayer

It is helpful to start and close each meeting with prayer. At the beginning it helps focus everyone's attention on the purpose of the session, and helps them to be aware of God's presence. At the end of the evening it is good to turn any problems which have been unearthed into prayer, and to ask for God's help in clarifying or carrying out the plans made during the session. If you do not feel able to make your own prayers up on the spot, a prayer which can be read aloud is included at the beginning and end of each session. However, be aware that if you continue this throughout the weeks you will severely inhibit anyone else who may otherwise have wished to pray aloud.

When you get to know your group you may find that they would like to pray openly together for a short period at the beginning or the end of the session. However:

- Do not force this upon the group.
- Do not pray round the group suggesting that members pray one after the other.
- Do not 'drop' on group members, asking them to pray there and then.

There are good reasons for this:

1 Some people feel very threatened by having to pray aloud and will opt out of the group rather than put themselves at risk of doing this.

2 Not everyone can make prayers up on the spot and they feel foolish if they dry up or put something badly.

3 The fact that some people can pray fluently undermines the confidence of those who are less able. Feeling they have to match such 'polished fluency' can be very stressful.

If you pray yourself rather than reading the suggested prayer from the session notes, make sure you keep the prayers short. Be relevant, keep to the point, and use everyday language.

At the end of sessions you may feel it appropriate to invite anyone who wishes to, to offer a short prayer, maybe just one sentence. If you do this, make it clear that you will allow a few moments' silence in which anyone who wants to pray is free to do so, and that you will close the time of prayer with a final prayer. Having such a framework will give group members a sense of security – they know what is going to happen – and so make it easier for them to participate.

Keeping a register

At the back of this book you will find a register sheet on which to record the names, addresses and phone numbers of group members, as well as a record of their attendance each week. This is helpful for a number of reasons:

1 It provides the information you need should you have to get in touch with any group member between meetings.

2 It helps you to keep track of individual members' attendance. If one of the group drops out at a certain stage the register will highlight this and point out the need for you to enquire after them. It also gives you a *constant reminder* to take a pastoral interest if you failed to do so when a member's absence was first noted!

3 It provides you with a record of individual members' attendance patterns which can be very useful when setting up new groups. A group should not contain only irregular attenders or the leader will find himself or herself in a difficult and discouraging position.

4 It will provide you with an accurate attendance figure – rather than what you think it is! The actual figure may be so different to what you imagine it to be that it can give you food for thought. It might show interesting variations from group to group and session to session which may also prompt you to do a little productive research on the reasons for it being so. The follow-up group leaders' session will provide an opportunity for discussing these figures.

If someone does miss a session it is good to enquire after them. If no one else in the group knows why they are absent, make a point of telephoning them or visiting before the next session. It may be that they simply need encouragement to come and the assurance that their presence in the group is valued. They may need some practical help in order to be able to come, such as someone to babysit. Do what you can to help arrange this. On the other hand, they may simply feel that the group is 'not for them'. Accept their decision lovingly, and make sure you do not, thereafter, drop all contact with them. Do not take the decision personally, feeling that you must have failed as a group leader; this is probably far from the truth.

Coffee and chat
It will be helpful to make sure that your host

knows exactly when coffee is required. Stress that the refreshments are not to be a mini-feast with cakes, sandwiches and biscuits. The only alternatives to coffee should be tea and squash. If hosts do provide a 'feast' it is very difficult for them to draw back on subsequent weeks because they will feel bad about offering less. It can also be very costly over the weeks and can prevent other people from offering to host the meeting because they will conclude that it involves giving a weekly 'feed'.

Change of leadership

It is a good principle for the same leader to lead each week, especially the first three or four sessions, so that the group establishes a sense of identity. If you are ever unable to attend a group meeting you should ask a group member, well in advance, to take your place. For the sake of continuity it is best to choose a deputy from among the group rather than someone from outside. If for any reason you cannot lead your group and you do not have a deputy, let your church leader or house group co-ordinator know as soon as possible.

1

One of the crowd

Zacchaeus

Preparation

Read through the leader's notes on pages 8–25, especially the section on how the 'Welcome' is to be carried out at this first group meeting. Each member of the group will need a pen and a piece of paper for the 'Why not?' exercise.

Arrive early and select the most 'advantageous' chair from which to lead the group; that is, one where everybody in the room will be able to see you.

Welcome each member by name as they arrive. Give people a chance to talk and chat before starting the group meeting. This is a time when people are able to get to know each other. It might be an idea to have a few spare Bibles around in case one of the members of the group has forgotten to bring their's along. If someone has not brought a Bible DO NOT FORCE A COPY ON THEM IN CASE THEY ARE NOT CONFIDENT READERS. They may prefer at this stage to sit and watch what happens before joining in. Leave the spare copies in an accessible place, point them out when the Bible reading comes around and leave the initiative with them to take a copy if they wish to.

Check that your host knows when tea, coffee and squash should appear and that he or she is providing only this and not a mini feast.

Welcome

After giving the group time to talk informally:

- Thank the host for letting the group use his or her home.
- Restate the arrangements for meeting: time, place, how many sessions there will be and what the series is called.
- State the aims of the series of meetings:

    1 To help group members get to know one another better.

    2 To take a look at some Bible characters and compare certain things they experienced with similar situations today.

    3 To see if there is anything practical we should do as a result of our discussion.

    4 To help us to see what part each of us can play in the life of our church and the kingdom of God in general.

- Explain that each session will be made up of the following:

    1 Informal conversation.

    2 A question-and-answer discussion on a Bible passage.

    3 A decision on what we might be able to do in the light of that discussion. On the following week we will take time to see if the ideas we came up with worked or not and what we learned from our efforts.

    4 A 'Why not?' fun exercise.

    5 A prayer to open and close with.

    6 A cup of coffee or tea at the end of the evening.

Introductions

After giving these brief details, introduce yourself to the group, and introduce each member of the group. Give their name and a little bit of personal information about each of them. Round off each introduction asking if you have got your facts right about them and by asking what name they would like to be known by in the group. An example of how this exercise works in practise is given in the group leader's notes on pages 12–14.

Prayer

Now we have begun to get to know each other, let's pray and ask God to be with us each time we meet together.

'Lord, at the outset of this series of meetings we ask for your help.

'Help us to get to know each other better. Help us to understand more about you and about ourselves as we look at the lives of people in the Bible. Help us to trust each other enough to share what we discover, as we begin to understand one another more. Amen.'

Bible reading

This series is called 'People like us' and the title of our first session is 'One of the crowd.' We are going to jump straight into our first Bible reading and discussion. What we are going to be thinking about in particular is being unwelcome, being given the 'cold shoulder'. We will look at how we might exclude people from our company, and at how we might feel if we were the person being shut out.

If you have not brought a Bible along, but would like to follow as I read the passage, there are some spare copies here. It is **Luke 19**, **verses 1 to 10**, which starts on page . . .

The passage describes what happened to one man who knew what it was to be ignored and excluded.

His name was Zacchaeus. People had a very good reason for excluding him: he was a traitor in their eyes. At the time of Christ Israel was oppressed by the occupying armies of Rome. The Israelites hated the Romans and tried to have as little contact with them as they could. Zacchaeus, however, was an Israelite who worked for the Romans – collecting taxes from his fellow Israelites to keep the Roman army in new boots.

Read Luke 19:1–10 aloud, yourself. Never read round the group or drop on someone unexpectedly to read aloud. If you have not already done so, read the section, 'Use of the Bible' in the 'Leader's notes' on pages 14–16.

Why not?

Draw a picture

Being the first session you should keep the 'Why not?' very light. All the 'Why nots?' are designed to help your group feel relaxed and comfortable and should prepare the atmosphere for friendly and helpful discussion on the subject which follows.

For this session, ask each person to take two minutes to sketch the place or places where they feel most insecure. You will need to provide them with paper and pens. Give them some examples to start them thinking, eg bus stops, the church, the DHSS office, crowded shops, open spaces.

Emphasise that they should not spend too much creative talent on their drawings – they have only two minutes after all! At the end of two minutes ask volunteers to hold up their 'Leonardo da Vincis' and to explain where it is that they feel most insecure.

Discussion

Attempt as many questions as you can this week without running over time. Keep the discussion moving and avoid spending all the time on one or two questions.

1 Zacchaeus was obviously interested in Jesus. If someone came along to church to see what Christianity was all about, how could we prevent them feeling excluded?

Let the group think this over before going on to the following suggestions. Give people time to find the verses, but read them out yourself.

(a) What do the following verses suggest we might do?

- Matthew 25:35; Hebrews 13:2.

(b) James 2:1–4 warns how wrong attitudes towards newcomers can cause people to exclude some and favour others. What wrong attitudes might cause people in our church to respond badly to newcomers?

- 'I don't know you; I only speak to the people I know.'
- 'They are not my age group; I only talk to people of my own age.'
- 'They don't look like my sort; they look poor/scruffy/middle class/working class.'
- 'They're black/brown/white, so I wouldn't know what to say to them.'

2 Why do you think the people at Jericho shunned Zacchaeus and excluded him?

3 What do you think Zacchaeus and Jesus both meant by what they said in verses 8 and 9?

4 If Jesus is the one who goes out to look for the lost, why do we need to bother about them?

Action

After each of these discussions we are going to try to think of some practical response to our discussion, so let me ask you what practical steps we can take as a group, this Sunday, to make newcomers and visitors to our church feel welcome.

Give the group time to talk this one over; people may find it easier to talk if you divide them into twos. Then ask for their suggestions. Select the most popular or most workable idea and suggest that this Sunday they all have a go at doing whatever has been suggested. If the group fails to come up with any ideas you could make the following suggestion:

What if we all try to watch our own reactions to those we sit next to in church, whom we don't know, and ask ourselves, 'What holds me back from talking to them and getting to know them?' If possible, let's try to make some contact with them by shaking hands or by talking to them.

Prayer

Pray yourself, or use the following prayer. DO NOT POUNCE ON ONE OF THE GROUP TO PRAY. If you have not already done so, refer to the notes on prayer in the Leader's notes, pages 22–23.

'Thank you, Lord, for all that our discussion has taught us about ourselves and about our attitudes to people in our church whom we do not know. Help us to be able to reach out to them with the warmth of your love. Amen.'

Coffee and chat

If you find that your host is forgetful about putting the kettle on in good time, remind him or her to do so at a suitable time. It might be most appropriate for this to be done just before the closing time of prayer, or during the 'Action' section.

Do not forget to fill in the register on page 96.

2

Putting your foot in it

Peter

Preparation

Arrive early and, once again, select a seat where you will be visible to the rest of the group. If you feel that group members did not get to know each other very well last week, give each person, as they arrive, a large sticky label on which they can write their names. (Make sure that the sticky labels will not damage clothes.)

Welcome

After giving the group time to talk and chat for a few minutes welcome them and explain as follows about the labels:

If you are like most people, remembering names probably won't come easily to you. It can be very embarrassing to forget the name of a person to whom you have just been introduced. So to save our blushes we will write on our labels the name by which we would like the group to call us. Please write it as large as you can. If, however, you find that you can't see what has been written on a label, don't feel embarrassed to ask that person to remind you of his or her name.

What not?

Introduce each other

> Introduce the following exercise. It is meant to be fun, so keep it light-hearted. You will need either a watch to time 30-second periods, or – if you really want to hot things up – a box of matches! The aim is for the whole group to come up with as much information on each person in the group as they can remember from last time. Focus on one person at a time. If you are using the watch, appoint a time-keeper who will tell the group when they can start pooling all the information they can remember about that person – and when to stop. If you decide to use matches, the time-keeper (or each group member in turn) strikes a match. While it is burning the group members can speak; time is up when the match gets too hot to handle. This can be great fun, but it is essential that the person striking the match has a plate or metal tray to drop the match onto when it gets too hot to hold, just in case you set the whole group on fire. Move as quickly as you can round the group. Speed is the secret of success.

Here's a short, fun exercise to help us remember some of the things we found out about each other last week. When I call out a group member's name see how much information you can remember about him or her, and call it out. The idea is to get as many pieces of information in as you can before thirty seconds is up.

Prayer

> Pray yourself or use the following prayer.

'Father, we thank you for your love which welcomes us into your family as your children. Thank you that you know all there is to know about each of us yet you continue to love us. As we get to know more about each other through these times of fellowship and discussion, help us to accept each other in the same spirit of love with which you have accepted us. Amen.'

Report back

Last time we agreed to watch our own reactions to those we sat by in church and to ask ourselves, 'What holds me back from talking to those around me whom I don't know?' We also suggested that we should try talking to one such person. What conclusions did we come to and how did we get on?

Bible reading

We are going to look at another character in this series on people like us, with whom we may have lots of things in common. His name is Peter and the title of the session is 'Putting your foot in it.' We are going to look at one incident in particular which is recorded in **Luke 22:54–62**. Let's read it together. It's on page. . . If anyone else would like to read the passage at future meetings please do so! But you'll have to volunteer or I'll end up doing it each week – I'm not going to press-gang anyone into reading! If, of course, you'd like to have a little time to prepare it, then let me know and I'll give you a note of the verses in good time.

The passage starts with Jesus being arrested and taken away for trial.

Read Luke 22:54–62.

Discussion

Remember that you do not have to answer all the questions, so watch your time and be selective.

1 If you were Peter, how do you think you would be feeling, standing there by the courtyard fire?

2 Sometimes we are asked about our faith by our friends or people we work with. How do you feel when this happens?

3 Do you think Christians should talk with other people about what Jesus means to them? What advice would you give a Christian trying to do this?

4 Why do you think Peter denied any knowledge of Jesus? Do you think people avoid sharing their faith with others for similar reasons? If so, what might those reasons be?

5 How can we share our faith with other people without actually telling them about it? Other passages in the New Testament give us some clues here. Let's look up some verses and think about practical ways in which we can apply the advice today.

> Do not forget to give out the page numbers where these verses are to be found. Read out the verses to the group.

● Matthew 5:16. Can you suggest three or four ways in which we could share our faith in the way Jesus tells us to here?
● 1 Peter 3:1–2. How does Peter advise the Christian wife to go about winning her non-Christian husband for Christ? Could Peter's advice be applied more widely – maybe to relationships other than husband and wife? If it could, which relationships, and how?
● 1 Peter 3:15–17. Peter does then go on to encourage his readers to talk about Jesus to people

who don't know him. But what advice does he give? How can we apply it today?

6 Can you suggest, maybe from our discussions so far, how we could set about the task of sharing our faith with others in our area? Is there something we could do as a group?

Action

Encourage the group to adopt one or two of the suggestions made in answer to question six and have a go at trying them out. If your group does not come up with any ideas that could be worked on easily by next time you could suggest they invite someone to come along with them to church next Sunday, or one Sunday in the near future. You could spend some time thinking about who they might invite and how they might go about it.

Prayer

Pray yourself, or use the following prayer:

'Lord, help us to live more easily than we have in the past with the responsibility of sharing our faith with others. Help us to have a winsome and natural way of going about it. Help us to see how our lives and the things we do for others can speak about you. Help us by your Spirit to reach out to those around us with the Good News of Jesus and to have the joy of seeing some of them come to know you. Amen.'

Coffee and chat

Do not forget to fill in the register on page 96.

3

Practical parenting
Mary

Preparation

Take a good look at the evening's plan before you go to the group meeting, so that you are familiar with its contents and will be able to lead it through with confidence. You may not have enough time to cover all the questions in the 'Discussion' section so decide beforehand which ones you will definitely ask and which ones you will leave out if you find that time has gone.

Welcome

Once again, arrive in good time to welcome the group members as they arrive. Look out for those who are not mixing very well and introduce them to members of the group to whom they have not yet talked. Most people find it helpful to have time to chat before the session begins. It allows people to get to know each other in an informal atmosphere and helps them to be less wary of each other once the meeting starts.

Prayer

Pray yourself, or use the following prayer. Allow half a minute's silence between each sentence:

'Let us pray.
'Let us pause for a moment or two of silent prayer and, in the silence, let us open our hearts and minds to the Spirit of God.' (Pause.)
'Help us Lord, at the end of this busy day, to open our hearts to your presence and peace.' (Pause.)
'Help us, Holy Spirit, to open our minds to hear what you have to say to us from your word. (Pause.) Amen.'

Report back

At our last get-together we thought about ways in which we could share our faith with others. And we decided we would . . .

> Recap on what the group decided to do, asking how things worked out. Show appreciation of any attempts that were made, even if they met with failure.

Bible reading

The title of this week's session is 'Practical parenting' and the character we are going to look at is Mary, the mother of Jesus. We are going to concentrate our attention on the needs of mothers and ask ourselves some very searching questions. The passages we are going to read are well-known as they form part of the Christmas story. They are **Luke 1:26–38** on page. . . and **Luke 2:1–7** on page . . .

> In case your group members forget to bring their Bibles, have a few spare copies handy. Remember not to assume that everyone will want to take a copy, but invite people to use one if they wish to.

Why not?

Do some quick thinking

The chips are frying away in the pan, when the baby starts to cry. Just then the telephone and the door bell ring. The neighbour is shouting over the fence that she sees your toddler at the upstairs window. In the confusion, the repair man cuts his finger badly on a knife and the little boy you look after crawls towards the flight of concrete steps which lead down to your garden below.

Discussion

1 Because Mary was the mother of Jesus she is often regarded as different from other women. Yet she was a very ordinary young mother. With the help of the person next to you, make a short list of all the things Mary has in common with the mums of today.

After a couple of minutes take time with the whole group to listen to the observations of the smaller groups, taking one observation from each group to begin with.

2 Mary was being called to be the mother of Jesus. It was a very special 'calling' for a very special task. Although the Bible does not talk of motherhood in general in this way there are those who feel that bringing up a family has this sense of 'calling' about it. How helpful or unhelpful do you think it is to hold this view today? To what would such a 'calling' be? To be a caring mother? A keeper of the house and garden? Instructor and teacher of a

Christian way of life? Counsellor, administrator of discipline and fair play?

3 If the mother of a young family also had a job outside the home, what particular difficulties do you think she might face? If you have been in this situation or know anyone who has, how were some of the problems overcome?

4 Many people think that if God is involved in something, nothing will go wrong. However, within most young families there are times when everything seems to go wrong. At such times it is easy for a mum to think God has abandoned her and that he is no longer in control of events. With the help of the same partner you worked with in question 1 make a list of all the things that went wrong for Mary and Joseph leading up to, and after, the birth of Jesus. When you have made a list share your findings with the wider group.

> Four suggestions are given below to guide discussion.
> • Caesar Augustus called for a taxation census which involved Mary in a very long journey on the back of a donkey;
> • There was no room anywhere when they arrived at Bethlehem;
> • Jesus was finally born in temporary makeshift accommodation;
> • They ended up as refugees in Egypt.

5 What do Mary's and Joseph's experiences have to say to committed Christians about the reality of family life today and about God's involvement in difficult circumstances?

6 Because we sometimes think of Mary as a 'special' mum, we can think that she must have been the 'perfect' mum. When we compare ourselves with the way other people cope with their families we can easily begin to feel failures. What makes you, as an individual, feel this way and what causes mothers particularly to feel inadequate? What advice would you give to someone who is suffering from feelings of failure and inadequacy because of comparing themselves unfavourably with someone else?

7 Mothers can be very isolated from other people, and feel trapped by their children. How can churches become more aware of this? What practical suggestions can we, as a group, put forward to our church leadership for improving its ministry to mums? Is there anything we, as a group, can do to help? What, for instance, can we do to support mothers whose husbands are not Christians?

> Note down any ideas that are suggested and pass them on to the minister or one of the leaders of your church, for them to consider. You may be able to follow up some of the ideas as a group, so do this in the action section.

Action
> Take up one of the practical suggestions in answer to question 7 and pass the others on to the minister or church leaders. It might help to come to this group meeting with one or two practical suggestions of your own in case the group does not come up with anything. Share your suggestions with them and it may help to spark their thinking.

Prayer
> Give the members of your group an opportunity to pray a short sentence prayer at this point. After allowing a few moments for those who wish to pray to do so, pray yourself or use the prayer below to indicate the prayer time is over.

One or two of you might like to say a short sentence prayer out loud as part of this closing time of prayer. I will allow a few moments for anyone who would like to pray to do so, then I will close with a final prayer. If anyone wants to pray aloud feel free to do so now and we will all say 'Amen' after it.

Let us pray. (Silence.)

'Lord, help us to appreciate the strains and stresses which others face in their lives. Forgive us that we are so often preoccupied with the problems of our own stage of life that we become blind and insensitive to the needs of others. Help us as your people to grow in love for one another so that we learn to show our love in practical caring. Amen.'

Coffee and chat

Do not forget to fill in the register on page 96.

4

Feeling small

Gideon

Preparation

Remember to take paper and pens for the 'Why not?' exercise.

The first part of the ability- or gift-spotting exercise starts this week. For this you will need one large stone for each group member, and several felt tip pens. If you cannot find stones of a reasonable size you could easily cut out stone shapes, about the size of a house brick, from coloured card. This is usually obtainable in art shops or stationery suppliers. The idea of using stones or stone-shaped card, links in with 1 Peter 2:5 where Peter describes believers in Christ as 'living stones', which are being built together to form God's church. You will also need a 'strong box' or 'swag bag' to keep the stones in, between sessions.

If you have not done so already, you should also talk to your minister or church leaders about the possibility of holding a special service for the offering of the congregation's gifts and abilities. You will also need to talk over with the minister ways in which gifts and abilities identified and offered during this exercise can be used in the church. (See pages 92–93.)

Once again, you may not have time to discuss all the questions in the 'Discussion' section, so read them through before the session, selecting the ones to which you feel the group will respond.

Welcome

Let the group relax and chat before starting the session but watch that this part of the programme does not get longer each week. If new members join the group introduce them in the same way as you introduced group members in the first session.

Prayer

Give the members of your group an opportunity to pray a short sentence prayer to open this session. At the end pray yourself or use the prayer below. This will also indicate that the prayer time is over.

Let's pray together. One or two of you might like to pray a short sentence prayer during this prayer time. I will wait a few moments for any one to pray who wants to and then I will close the prayer time with a prayer. You can pray silently or, if you prefer, say a short prayer out loud. Feel free to do this in the silence that follows and we will all say 'Amen' after it.

Let us pray. (Silence.)
'Lord, thank you for the way in which these group meetings are bringing us closer to one another and deepening our understanding of one another. We thank you that the characters we have looked at in this series remind us that you are able to use ordinary people in your service. Help us to see exactly how we can be of service to you. Amen.'

Report back

If the group came up with suggestions for action at the end of the last meeting (other than those you were to pass on to church leaders) find out how they got on in practice. Encourage the group to attempt some form of positive action if they have not done so already; and encourage those whose efforts met with little or no success. It is also important

Last time we came up with the following suggestions for practical action . . . How did you get on?

Bible reading

This session is called 'Feeling small', and we will be putting the spotlight on Gideon. Many of us have things in common with him. One thing he particularly suffered from was a deep sense of inferiority. When God called him, asking him to do a particular 'up front' job, he was very reluctant and needed lots of reassurance before he was willing to say yes. It's interesting to see how capable he actually turned out to be in the service of God. Let's see what we can learn from this reluctant leader.

The part of the story we are going to look at is found in the book of Judges in the Old Testament. It is **Judges chapter 6, verses 1–6 and 11–16**. It can be found on page . . .

Why not?

Read a letter

'Dear God,

I am so sorry that I let you down again last week at church. When the Minister asked me to read the Bible in the service next week I just had to say 'No'. You know that I find it difficult to do things in front of others; they are so much more spiritual than I am and know you so much better. I feel such a hypocrite! Please don't ask me to do anything too hard as I don't think a person such as me could cope. Someone like Peter would be better. He's great at speaking and talks naturally to people. I know you like using him.

God, you know my limitations so please be nice to me . . .'

1 Why do we sometimes feel so inadequate when we try to please God?

2 What is it inside us that makes us think somebody else can do it better?

3 Why do we come up with excuses for not doing something we feel we should, even if we would really like to do it?

Discussion

If you are to leave time for the first part of the gift- and ability- spotting exercise, it may not be possible to use all the questions given below, so keep an eye on the clock. For this part of the discussion divide the group into units of two or three then ask them to discuss questions 1, 2 and 3 within these small groups.

1 What sort of person does Gideon appear to be in this passage? Try to list as many of his characteristics as you can.

2 This question is just for discussion in our small groups; we will not be sharing our assessment with the whole group:

Are there any ways in which you feel Gideon is like you, or ways in which you feel he was very different?

3 God saw Gideon's potential even though Gideon did not. God saw that Gideon could become a 'warrior'. Why do you think Gideon was so blind to his own potential? Could the same be true of us?

4 How do you think we can discover our potential to serve God?
● In what ways can other Christians help us to discover our potential?
● When might it help to have a go and find out from experience?
● What other means might there be?

5 Gideon was a man who needed a lot of reassurance and encouragement. Let's look at a few of the verses in this passage and try to see how that reassurance and encouragement came to him.
● 6:22–24
● 6:36–40

- 7:10–11, 15–16

  If the group have difficulty coming up with ideas, ask them to think about God's words, about his actions or signs, and about circumstances and timing. (Each of the above references deals with one of these.)

6 Can you think of a time when you felt God was encouraging or reassuring you (or someone you know) in one of these ways? Describe for the group what happened.

If you are not aware of any such occasion, how do you think God is most likely to encourage his people today? (You may like to see what 1 Thessalonians 5:11,14 and Hebrews 10:25 have to say.)

7 What do you suppose Gideon was thinking in verse 13? Do you ever think like this?
- If you do, what causes you to think like it?
- What sort of feelings come to the surface when you do think like this?

  If group members say that they feel angry, guilty, faithless, or as though they are not good Christians, it would probably be helpful to discuss a little more fully why they feel this way.

- Why do you think God did not reject Gideon as 'unsuitable' for thinking like this?

  Point out that it is not wrong to be angry at an unjust situation; Jesus was angry when he saw the Temple being misused (Mark 11:15–17), and the Old Testament prophets were often angered and saddened by the selfishness of their society. When we feel like this God may want us to do something about the situation we find. If Gideon was angry about his people being oppressed by the Midianites, God could have used the strength of that emotion to work some good.

Action

Over the next few weeks we are going to try to help each other discover particular abilities, talents and gifts that God has given us and which he may be able to use in a special way in his service. We may already be aware of certain abilities which we possess and which God can use; we may not be so aware of others. We must realise from the outset that some of us may have more abilities than others but we all have some gift or ability God can use. We also need to take note of the fact that we may not know each other well enough to be able to compile a complete list of each individual's abilities. This sort of list can be a useful servant, but a bad master: don't be bound for the rest of your life by what does or does not appear on it! Always be seeking to add to it.

On the table is a pile of fairly large stones. Each of us will select one and write our name on it with the felt tip pen provided. Then we will hand round the stones, each of us writing on the stone one particular ability, talent or gift which the person has whose name appears on the stone. If you don't know someone well enough to write anything about them yet just pass the stone on and give some thought to it between now and the next group meeting. Next time you might be able to write something down. There are no marks for spelling or handwriting, and you are free to draw a person's gift rather than write it down.

> Please treat this exercise with a little light-heartedness. It is meant to be an enjoyable, not a palm-sweating, exercise! Once the stones have been written on, collect them up in a 'strong box' or 'swag bag' and make it clear that you will be looking after it. Assure people that you will not leave their stones lying around, open to the gaze of anyone who may be passing! Explain that they will be used, if group members

wish it, as part of an act of dedication at the end of the series, possibly in a service of dedication in church. Encourage them to copy out the items on their stones for their own reference.

Prayer

Pray yourself or use the following prayer:

'Thank you, Lord, for your patience with us. Thank you that you are a God who encourages us to serve you. Help us to step out in faith as Gideon did even though we might doubt our own abilities and be afraid of what other people might think or say. As we do so, help us to become stronger in faith and more able to serve you. Amen.'

Coffee and chat

If your host is providing more than tea, coffee and squash, tactfully remind him or her that it would really be better to keep to just these items. Point out that, although his or her generosity is genuinely appreciated, it can have the effect of making others in the group feel inadequate and so prevent them from hosting groups in the future. If your host really enjoys providing feasts and perhaps feels it is one of the few gifts he or she has, invite him or her to organize and host an 'end of series' supper for the group's last meeting. Make sure first, though, that this is how the rest of the group would like to conclude the series. Also encourage the host to accept the help and contributions of group members.

Do not forget to fill in the register on page 96.

5

With a little help from my friends

Dorcas

Preparation

Group members will need the stones again on which they began to write last week, so do not forget to take the 'strong box' or 'swag bag' with you to the meeting. They will also need the felt tip pens. Bring a variety of Bible translations to the meeting this week as the group will need to refer to them in answer to the first question in the discussion. The RSV, NIV and GNB would be good versions to use.

There are several readings so, if you do have keen readers in your group, it would be good to share out the load. Remember to ask each reader well before the meeting, so that they can take a good look at their passage. Some of the names in Acts 9 sound a bit strange and need a little practice.

If you are going to attempt the 'Why not?' exercise you will also need a piece of paper for each group member and a large sheet of paper for yourself.

Welcome

Arrive early enough to greet each group member as they arrive. By now each member of the group should have met every other member of the group. If there are still members

Prayer

Let's pause for a moment or two of silent prayer. We'll pray for one another in the light of the things we have begun to learn about each others' life and circumstances. I will make suggestions for prayer, and will leave a few moments for silence after each for our prayers.

'Let us pray for the person on our left. (Pause.)
Let us pray for the person on our right. (Pause.)
Let us pray for one other group member. (Pause.)
Let us also pray for ourselves, remembering as we do so that God invites us to "cast all our cares upon him for he cares about us." (Pause.)
Lord, in your mercy, hear our prayer. Amen.'

Bible reading

Today's session is called, 'With a little help from my friends' and we are going to look at the common problem of feeling insignificant. A number of 'insignificant' characters in the Bible were used by God to great effect! One of them was the lady called Dorcas whom we read about in **Acts 9:36–43**. Let's read the passage; it's on page . . .

Why not?

Think of a person

Give each person a piece of paper and a pen.

First of all, we're going to try to think of as many 'insignificant' people as we can, people that we know. They are the ones that hardly anyone notices in the crowd; the ones who rarely speak in a group; the ones you have to think hard about when you wonder who is missing! Go through your memory bank, taking one such person at a time. Write down his or her first name (if you know it!), then write down one or two things about that person which shows he or she actually has a very important gift or ability which he or she uses to help other people. What are the valuable things which this person does, quietly and without drawing attention to himself or herself? If you prefer, you could draw pictures showing what the person does, rather than writing them down.

Give the group about three minutes to do this.

Now let's go round the group and, if we can, describe one of the people we have listed – but without mentioning names if someone else in the group is likely to know the person. Tell us about the contribution you realise he or she is making, quietly, behind the scenes.

As gifts and abilities are mentioned, jot them down on a large sheet of paper so that everyone can see. Spend a little time at the end discussing the range of gifts that have been mentioned. Are people surprised at the sorts of gifts that emerged? And their number?

Discussion

This session encourages the group to compare different translations of the Bible passage in order to come to a better understanding of it. If you have people in your group who are not confident readers, it might be better to ask just one or two people, whom you know will cope, to do the comparisons.

1 Let's look at verse 36 in a number of different translations.

● How do they describe Dorcas spiritually? What do you think the words mean and could they be used to describe us?

● What does this same verse (36) and the rest of the passage tell us about the way she lived her life?

● What do the various translations of verse 39 suggest she had made?

● How would you describe her gift; what name would you give it?

● Make a list of the effects that her life, and the using of her ability, had on the people around her. (See particularly verses 36, 38, 39, 42.)

2 Why do you think we often fail to see the potential of 'insignificant', everyday abilities in God's service?

3 Let's read John 6:5–11. It's on page . . .

You should have someone prepared to read this and the passage for question 4; otherwise read them yourself.

What simple steps led up to Jesus being able to use the lad's lunch? What might these steps suggest to us about the use of insignificant things?

If discussion is slow, you may like to suggest some of the following as possible answers to the first question:
● others saw what the lad had to offer;
● he was encouraged to offer what he had;
● he was willing to offer the little he had;

- he gave what he had to Jesus to use.

This will also give the group some ideas from which to answer the second part of the question.

4 Let's get another perspective on this by reading Jesus' parable about three servants who were entrusted with different sums of their master's money. It's in Matthew 25:14–30, which starts on page . . .

Read this to the group, then ask:

What particular point do you think Jesus is making when he describes the servant who had the smallest amount of money?

Try to avoid getting bogged down in issues of reward and punishment. Rather help the group to see that God expects us to use what he has given us, even if that might be very little.

Report back and action

Over the past week we have been thinking of gifts and abilities we could write on one another's stones. I'm going to pass them round again for you to write down any other things you may have thought of. Try to use one word to describe the gift or ability you have in mind so that the stone does not get too full too quickly! When your own stone comes back to you don't think you must be superman or superwoman if there's a lot on it; and certainly don't be disappointed if there's not as much on it as you had hoped! If there's not very much on your stone it will be because we don't really know one another very well. Perhaps we have not had enough contact with each other outside of these evenings to see each other's gifts in action in other settings. However, when your stone does reach you, turn it over and write on the reverse side some of the gifts and abilities you feel you have to offer.

Prayer

Once again, give the members of your group an opportunity to pray a short 'sentence-prayer'. After you have given a few moments for anyone to pray who wishes to do so, pray yourself or use the prayer below. This will again indicate that the prayer time is over.

One or two people might like to say a short sentence prayer out loud as part of this closing time of prayer. I will allow a few moments for this then I will close with a final prayer. If anyone would like to pray aloud, feel free to do so now and we will all say 'Amen' to it.

Let us pray. (Pause.)

'Lord, we thank you that you use our insignificant gifts and abilities, as well as the more obvious ones. Thank you that we can bring your love and help to those around us, through using the gifts you have given us. Help us not to think of those gifts as being unimportant, because that will only restrict your power and our potential in your service. Help us to simply offer what we have to you, and let you use us in whatever way you think best. Amen.'

Coffee and chat

Do not forget to fill in the register on page 96.

6

In the pits

Elijah

Preparation

If any of the group have been absent, make tactful enquiries about them in case they are unwell. If they have not let you or anyone else in the group know why they are no longer coming, the reason may well be something to do with the group itself! If no one knows why they have been absent, you should go round to visit them yourself. Be prepared to accept any comments they may want to make about the group and to put right anything that is causing unnecessary problems. Assure them that they are being missed and encourage them, if it seems right, to give it another go. In certain situations it might be possible to mobilize the group to give whatever practical support is needed by someone who is finding it difficult to keep up attendance.

For the 'Why not?' section you will need an A4 sheet of paper, with a triangle drawn on it (see page 60), for each member of the group. This may be photocopied from the book.

Remember to select in advance the key questions that you will ask during the 'Discussion' time.

Prayer

'Father, we thank you that through making us part of your body you have given to each of us gifts and abilities you want to use for the good of others. As we try to discover what these gifts are and how we can best use them, deliver us from fear which can so easily put us off taking the first step. Keep us from looking on the gifts we have as being too insignificant to be worth offering to you. Amen.'

Report back and Action

Before we go any further this week let's take one more look at the stones we have been writing on over the last couple of weeks. Are there any more gifts and abilities we would like to add to our own list or to someone else's?

> Give the group time to take another look at the stones and add to them. If there are some individuals who are struggling to collect items on theirs, you should be prepared to add some more as a result of your own further thinking about each person.

Take a good look at your own list of gifts and abilities so that you can give some thought and prayer to them over the coming week. Let's pray about which of these gifts we could start experiment with first. Let's ask God to show us at least one gift or ability which we can begin to use in his service in some way. Next time we meet we will share with each other any conclusions we have come to.

Bible reading

Once again the reading has some long names in it, so read it yourself unless you have an experienced reader who would not mind reading it to the group, or unless you have asked someone in advance to prepare it.

We are going to look at another Old Testament character and see what we have in common with him. His name is Elijah and the title of our session is 'In the pits.' The particular incident in his life we are going to look at occurred after he had seen God win a great victory over the prophets of the heathen god called Baal at Mount Carmel. Elijah had challenged the prophets of Baal to prove that their god was real. So both parties set up an altar and placed a slaughtered animal on it. Then each group in turn called on their God to send miraculous fire to set it alight. Nothing happened when the prophets of Baal called on him, though they tried for long enough. When Elijah asked God to send fire to burn up his sacrifice, it came, and it was obvious which of the two 'Gods' was the real one. Let's read what happened next. The passage we need to turn to is **1 Kings 19:1–15**, and it's on page . . .

Why not?

Describe the peaks and valleys

Give everyone a piece of paper (about A4 size) with a large triangle drawn on it. You can photocopy the illustration shown.

Write down at the peak of your triangle the things which really excite and uplift you; the things that make you 'float on cloud nine.'

Then at the base of the triangle write the things

which really get you 'down' and make you feel
depressed and annoyed.

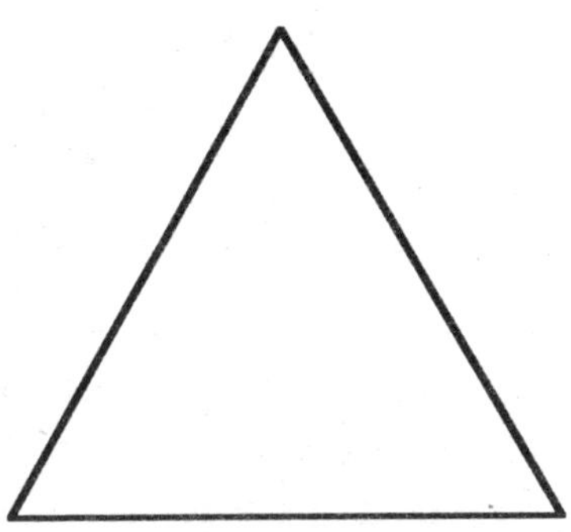

Discussion

1 Elijah had just seen God do great things in
answer to his prayers when suddenly a dark
shadow was cast over his life by Jezebel's threat to
kill him. Some Christians seem to live their lives
going between the spiritual 'highs' and the spiritual
'lows'. How would you describe a spiritual 'low'?
Is it true that if God is really at work in a person's
life he or she can usually expect temptation and
discouragement? What personal experiences of this
sort do you have that you could share with the
group?

2 How did Elijah react to his problem? Verses 3 and 4 mention a number of things.

Make sure that the following reactions are mentioned; but give the group plenty of time before adding any they have not spotted:
- he panicked;
- he ran away from the situation;
- he refused the company of his close companion, and tried to get as far away from other people as possible;
- he became gloomy about himself and what he had accomplished in his life;
- he felt he would be better off dead.

3 With the circumstances he was in and the pressure he was under, Elijah found a mixture of feelings welling up inside him. He was suddenly gripped by intense fear. He felt that he wanted to run away and hide from everybody and be on his own. He felt himself to be a total failure despite all that God had been able to do through him. He also felt like opting out of life altogether; he felt as though he just wanted to die. Perhaps today we would say Elijah was suffering from a form of depression.

Have you ever felt a similar collection of feelings rising to the surface at certain points in your life? If so, in what circumstances did you find this happening and how did you cope with them?

The following questions may prove useful in expanding the discussion, especially if people open up and share personal experiences.
- Were there any things which other people did that you found particularly helpful or particularly unhelpful at that time?
- Why do people find depression so hard to accept, especially some Christians?
- In what practical ways do you feel Christians could be of help to each other at such times?

4 Elijah finally arrived at Horeb, probably the mountain where God had given the ten commandments to Moses. There, God spoke to Elijah through a very interesting sequence of events. How did God speak to him? What do you think the story at this point has to say about the way in which God speaks to us today?

> It may be that there is a deliberate contrast here with the awesome and majestic way in which God spoke to Moses and Israel in this same place (see Exodus 19:16–19). He seems to have spoken to Elijah in a calm, quiet and gentle voice in the solitude of the cave, perhaps to emphasize that it was Elijah's love which God valued, not his fearful or grudging obedience.

5 Elijah seems to have heard an audible whisper on that occasion. How do we hear the voice of God speaking to us today?

> You may have got on to this in the last question, but if not, bring out the following suggestions: God may speak to us through the Bible, through the spoken word of the preacher or testimony, through reading Christian books, through personal experience, through circumstances, through the still small voice of inner intuition, through the gift of prophecy, through other gifts of the Spirit.

6 'The Lord said to me' or similar phrases have become very common in certain Christian circles today. Do you think that this phrase can be a slightly misleading overstatement and, if so, could you suggest a better way to describe the personal conviction or growing awareness that God might be trying to say or communicate something?

> If some people feel there is nothing wrong with claiming 'the Lord said ...' it may help to point out that it can be quite unhelpful to do so. If what a person has claimed in this way does not come about it may undermine someone else's faith in God. It would usually be better to say something like:
> * 'I have become increasingly aware that God is saying ...'

- 'I felt God was underlining this truth for me . . .'
- 'I feel that the Lord is trying to get across to me that . . .'
- 'It seemed to me as though God was saying . . .'

Then if this does not, in the long-run, appear to have been what God really was saying, everyone is clear that it was the person's understanding which was mistaken, not God changing his mind or talking nonsense.

Prayer

Pray yourself or use the prayer that follows:

'Lord, help us to be more understanding of those who find themselves feeling useless or depressed like Elijah. Help us to be of practical help to them, especially by being more willing to listen than to offer simple answers. Help us to offer them supportive reassurance and the shelter of our company so that we can, in some small way, help to bear one another's burdens. Amen.'

A note for next week

It would help next week's discussion if we could all read Exodus chapters 3 and 4 before coming. Make a note of those chapters and try to find a few minutes between now and then to go through them.

Coffee and chat

Do not forget to fill in the register on page 96.

7

Who, me?!

Moses

Preparation

If the stones are to be used in an act of dedication, you will need to give to each person this week a completed list of their gifts and abilities – taken from the stones. This will be a record for them to keep. You may also like to compile a list of all the gifts or abilities written on the group's stones, for a permanent record. It might be worth taking a photocopy or carbon copy of the individual lists in case one of the group members loses theirs.

You will need to have some pieces of paper to hand for use later in the session.

Welcome

Be at the host's house early enough to greet each member as he or she arrives. Try to encourage conversation, particularly between group members who have not talked to each other very much so far.

Prayer

Give the members of your group an opportunity to pray a short sentence prayer to open the session this week. At the end pray yourself or use the prayer below.

One or two people might like to pray a short sentence-prayer to start our time together. I will wait a few moments for anyone to pray who wants to and then I will close the prayer time with a prayer. You can pray silently or say a short prayer out loud in the silence which follows, and we will all say 'Amen' at the end.

Let us pray. (Silence.)
'Jesus said "I am the light of the world. He who follows me will not walk in darkness but will have the light of life."

Lord Jesus, we thank you for the light of your presence in our world. We thank you that it is a light which helps us to see the truth, a light which helps us to understand ourselves and a light which helps us to be conscious of the needs of others. As we think and talk about your word help us to discover fresh insights about ourselves and those around us. Help us, too, to see how we can reach out to others in practical ways which show your love. Amen.'

Bible reading
The reading which forms the basis of our discussion comes from Exodus. I hope you had a chance to read chapters 3 and 4 for yourself as we are only going to be able to read **Exodus 3:1–12**. It's found on page . . .

Read the passage.

Why not?

Play 'Just a Minute'

Play 'Just a Minute', as in the well-known radio programme.

You could title it 'Just a Moses'! Volunteer four people who are probably the most outgoing of the group and tell them that they will be given a subject and that they will be expected to speak on it for just sixty seconds, without hesitation, deviation or repetition.

Naturally the others can interrupt a person if he or she fails to keep going or makes the mistakes of deviation or repetition.

Suggested topics:

- Holy Moses!
- Public speaking
- Racial hatred
- Slavery
- Excuses
- Family ties
- Any other subject related to the passage

Keep it light and see it as a good starter for your discussion. Do not pick anyone who you know would die if they were volunteered! The topics and the game will help introduce the subject of inadequacy, as well as introducing the areas in which Moses felt particularly inadequate.

Allow only seven to ten minutes for the game, or you will run out of time for the other sections.

Discussion

This session is called, 'Who, me?!' and it's about coping with feelings of inadequacy. Let's turn back to the passage we read a moment ago.

Once again time may not permit you to use all the questions in the discussion, so watch the clock and be selective. Make sure you leave ample time for the 'Report back' section.

1 What do you find striking or surprising about the way in which Moses was called?

2 Do you feel it is necessary to be 'called' to serve God, or is it sufficient to see the need and get involved if you have the abilities?

3 Moses had quite a number of reasons for not

getting involved in this project. Let's divide ourselves up into groups of two or three and make a list of all the reasons Moses had for not getting involved. When we have made our lists we will take a moment to report back to the rest of the group before moving on.

4 In our small groups, let's now make a list of the sort of reasons people give for not getting involved in the work of their church. When we have made our lists we will again spend a moment looking at the sort of things we have listed down.

How many of the reasons we have just listed are similar in some way or perhaps even identical to any of the reasons on our first list?

5 The one thing that kept Moses from responding with positive faith to God's call was his own feeling of inadequacy. 'O Lord, please send someone else to do it' is what he said in 4:13. Freeing his people from slavery was something Moses had longed to do years before, but his failure to do so then led him into doubt that he could do so now.

Read the part of Stephen's speech which talks about this: Acts 7:23–28.

What Moses meant was, 'Lord, send someone *better able* than me to do the job.' How common a feeling do you think this is among Christians today? What sort of church work in particular do you think is suffering because people have this feeling?

If your group thinks that feeling inadequate is a common and significant reason for people not getting involved in church work, ask them what could be done to resolve this situation. This may produce some ideas which can be followed up in the 'Action' section.

6 Moses proved to be a man with great leadership potential. How did this potential come to be realised and developed, and used to such great effect?

Some people will feel that training or teaching is the answer but in the case of Moses and many other biblical characters the training ground was their practical involvement. It was as Moses became involved in God's purposes that his potential developed and he became a great leader of God's people. Try to help your group to see that it is as we make what we have available to God that God can use it to great effect – like the lad who offered Jesus his lunch. It is also very important to point out that it is often after people become involved in the service of God that they begin to appreciate the need for some form of training and instruction in how to do better the things they are already involved in. This might be work with the youth club, Sunday school or worship group, preaching or working pastorally outside the church setting.

Report back

Ask each member of the group to take back their stone from the 'strong box' or 'swag bag.' Go on to explain from what follows exactly what you would like them to do at this point. Be aware that not every group member may want to take part in the exercise. Be sensitive to them and do not make it difficult for them to opt out. Sometimes those who are hesitant at this stage become more inclined to take part and have a go when they see other members of the group getting stuck in.

Last week we agreed to give thought and prayer to the gifts and abilities listed on our stones and to select one which we thought we could experiment with using. Which of the gifts on your list have you selected and how could you see it being used?

Ask each member in turn to report back on the gift they have selected. Try in each case to establish clear ideas of how it might be put to use. Do encourage any who are hesitant or unsure, but make it clear that if they would rather not comment they need only say 'pass' and the next person will carry on.

Let's set ourselves some clear goals for the coming week. Some of us will be happy to attempt to use the particular gift or ability straight away. Others of us may need to work out a few steps which have to be taken before we can actually start using our chosen gift or ability. Next week we can report back on our attempts to use our gifts.

Be careful that no one sets themselves unrealistic goals or they will only fail and feel discouraged. Some group members may need help from the rest in thinking out the preliminary steps they need to take; others will want to think about it on their own at home. Encourage each individual who takes part to set themselves a time limit by which they are going to complete their attempts at using their gift or ability. This helps to get people moving.

Action

If you or the group had a suggestion for action following on from question 5 in the discussion section, it can be taken up by someone at this stage. However, remember that this is not the prime objective of this session. It is more important that each group member is encouraged to see and use the gifts they have.

Prayer

Pray yourself or use the following prayer:

'Thank you, Lord, that you always use ordinary people in the service of your kingdom. Help us to stop hiding our gifts and abilities behind one excuse or another. Help us to come to terms with our own feelings of inadequacy so that we will not withhold our limited abilities because others seem to be more gifted than we are. We ask you now to open up for us opportunities during the week when we can put the gifts we have mentioned into active service for you. Amen.'

Coffee and chat

Do not forget to fill in the register on page 96.

8

Fractured families

Hannah

Preparation

The reading this week has some difficult names at the beginning of it, see note below on reading. If you are going to use the 'Family Influence Survey' you will need to photocopy one for each group member from the sample given in the text.

Welcome

Once again, keep your eyes open for opportunities to help group members meet and talk to one another as they arrive.

Prayer

Pray yourself or use the following suggestion:

Let us pause for a moment or two of silent prayer. I will suggest topics and leave space in between for our silent prayers. Then I will close with a prayer.

'Let us pray.

'We all have things that worry us and cause us concern. Let us bring them to mind and offer them to God in the silence.' (Pause.)

'We may also have other people's worries and concerns on our minds. Let us bring these to God in the silence too.' (Pause.)

'Lord, we offer these concerns and worries to you. Help us to lay them down now and to be open to all that your Spirit may have to say to us through our time together. Strengthen our faith and renew our trust. Amen.'

Report back

Last session some group members left with specific plans for how to use one of their gifts or abilities. Give these group members time now to report back on their successes or failures. Be sure to encourage those whose attempts met with failure or little success. In some cases it might be appropriate to encourage another try, or to suggest that a person uses another of the gifts or abilities on their list. Others may have come unstuck because they had not planned precisely enough how they were to set about using their gifts.

Some group members may have spent time thinking out the steps they needed to take before putting their chosen gift or ability into practice; so give them a chance to report back on this too. The group might like to suggest changes or give advice or encouragement at this point. It is helpful to agree on a date by which these steps need to be taken, or at least for when the task is to be accomplished. This helps to get people moving and to begin to see some progress.

Your group may also have taken up one of the suggestions they came up with in response to question 5 in last week's discussion. If they did, remember to let them report back on how they got on and agree another attempt or further action – whichever is felt necessary.

Bible reading

The person we are going to be looking at in this session is Hannah and the topic is 'Fractured families'. Her story is told in the first chapter of 1 Samuel. Let's read **1 Samuel 1 verses 1 to 28**.

Why not?

Assess some influences

Our 'family problems' are often caused by external influences rather than by problems in our family relationships. For instance, we try to live up to what other people expect of us. In addition, radio and TV programmes and the magazines which we allow into our lounge have enormous impact on our families. So here is a survey to help us pinpoint some of those influences.

Give each member of the group a copy of the chart shown on the next page. Ask them to take each source of 'influence' in turn and to tick one of the boxes next to it. These describe the degree of influence which that source has on their family.

Then go around the group, asking which things influence people 'a lot'. Dig a bit further with the group to find out how these things affect us. How far do they influence us against our will?

Discussion

1 Worship played an important part in the life of this family, judging by the fact that they made a journey to Shiloh each year for a special period of worship and sacrifice (verses 3, 19, 21, 28). But worshipping together also seemed to bring to the surface some underlying tensions in their family life.

A family influence survey

Influence on my family	Not at all	A little	A lot
Relatives			
Friends			
Television			
TV advertisements			
Films			
Radio			
Books			
Magazines			
Work friends			
Neighbours			
Weather			
Minister			
Church			
Bible			

(a) What problems can arise today for families that try to worship together? What sort of tensions might we expect to find bubbling to the surface?

(b) What practical suggestions can we make which will help families experiencing difficulties in this area?

2 Hannah was driven to tears by frustration and despair. She seems to have put up with an awful lot, year after year, and apparently without lashing out in revenge at the woman who teased her. She even seems to have resisted the temptation to sour Peninnah's relationship with Elkanah by telling him what was going on.

(a) Was this the best way to handle this sort of situation or should she have handled things differently? How do we think *we* would have handled this situation?

(b) What do we do with our own feelings of frustration and despair? Perhaps one or two of us could describe what has made us feel this way recently and what we have found helpful in coping with the situation.

Encourage the group to be as honest as they can in their responses. Some additional questions may help them think through the issues and come to some positive conclusions. For example:

When we ourselves are under tension or find we are becoming frustrated, do we sometimes take it out on others? Do we try to get other people into trouble to 'get our own back'? Do we try to shoulder all the pain ourselves, maybe to find we really cannot and so become crushed by it?

The group may need help to come up with constructive ways of coping with such situations. Ask how helpful the following have proved in their experience:

3 The Bible is not very clear about how much Elkanah knew of Hannah's anguish each year at Shiloh. But it does seem that this family had a communication problem.
(a) How difficult do we find it to communicate our feelings to other members of our family?
(b) What practical suggestions can we come up with for improving our ability to communicate with, and listen to, the others in our family?

4 Hannah found her way to the sanctuary and poured her heart out in honest prayer to God. It proved to be a very constructive way of releasing the tension that was building up inside her. Her prayer also actually changed her family situation.
(a) How do we react to reading this about her – does it encourage us, or depress us because we've tried to pray about this sort of situation and nothing has happened?
(b) What do we think of the fact that she prayed alone and not with her husband? How much of their prayer life should husbands and wives be able to share, if any?

5 While he was still very young Samuel came to know the Lord for himself.
(a) How big a part do you think is played by the local church in a young person's acceptance or rejection of their parent's faith?
(b) What can our church do to encourage the steady, committed Christian growth of its young people?

6 It seems that most children from Christian families go through a phase – some longer and more distressing than others – of rejecting the faith their parents hold. This is true, too, of the children of church leaders and ministers. We know that neither Eli's sons nor Samuel's followed in their father's footsteps. Some people put this down to the fact that such fathers are so busy with the work of caring for God's people that they have little or no time for their own families. Others suggest that, because of who their fathers are, the expectations of people around them as they grow up play an unhelpful part in the children's development.

What other reasons might there be, and what implications do they have for Christian parents today who are heavily involved in Christian work or leadership in the church?

Action

As an extension of the discussion on question 6 you might like to discuss some practical steps that can be taken to change unhelpful attitudes on the part of church congregations:

(a) towards those parents (especially if they are church leaders) of young adolescents who are going through 'the rebellious teenage stage', and

(b) towards the church's young people.

Encourage sensitivity on the part of the group in whatever they decide to do.

There may, alternatively, be other practical suggestions the group may like to take up which address other problems relating to family life that have been discussed this evening.

Special note:

If people have shared quite deeply during this session, ask the group to regard anything that was shared as being strictly confidential.

Encourage group members to call on each other during the week if they feel the need of extra support, prayer or

advice as they begin to work through some of these
situations.

Prayer

Give the members of your group an opportunity to pray a
short sentence prayer at this point. After you have given
them a few moments to pray, pray yourself or use the prayer
below to conclude the prayer time.

One or two people might like to say a short
sentence prayer out loud as part of this closing time
of prayer. I will allow a few moments for this,
then I will conclude with a final prayer. If anyone
would like to pray aloud, feel free to do so now.
We will all say 'Amen' after it.

'Let us pray.' (Silence.)

'Father, we have touched on many areas of
family life tonight which affect us deeply. Give us
courage to tackle the particular problems that have
been highlighted for each of us. Help us, with
love and sensitivity, to learn how to listen to and
understand the members of our families. Thank
you for the support of each other in this group.
Amen.'

Coffee and chat

Do not forget to fill in the register on page 96.

78

9

Pull the other one!

Thomas

Preparation

To help discussion in question 2 of the 'Discussion' section, write out some possible causes of doubt for the group to consider. You will need a large sheet of paper for this – the reverse side of a roll of wallpaper will do.

Welcome

By now group members may be mixing and talking freely as they arrive, but you may still be aware of individuals who have not had a chance to meet or talk to everyone in the group. Attempt to introduce them to another group member in this session. Arriving early may help you to do this.

Prayer

Pray yourself or use the following prayer:

'Father, we thank you for your word and the richness of its contents. We particularly thank you for the variety of characters we find in its pages and for the open and honest way in which their life stories are told. Help us to learn from their experiences, from their faults and failings as well as their strengths and successes. Help us to serve you in our own day as they did in theirs. Amen.'

Report back

Give those who have been attempting to use their gifts the chance to report back to the group on their progress – especially if there are those in your group who needed to work out steps to achieving their goals. It might also be the right time for some to choose a second gift or ability from their list to experiment with. Be sensitive towards those who are finding this exercise difficult; encourage them to keep going. It is important that you share your own experiences too, especially if your attempts have not proved very successful! Often the difficulties experienced by a leader are a positive form of encouragement to more hesitant members of the group. It shows that failure is not the end of the world, and that it affects leaders too! They know they are in good company and so should not feel so bad about their own poor showing.

If your group decided on a course of action in response to last week's discussion on 'Fractured families' make sure the group has a chance to report back and decide on further action if that is felt necessary.

Why not?

Call My Bluff

Play a variation of 'Call My Bluff'.

Give each person a piece of paper and a pen, then read out the words below and their definitions. For each definition, group members should write down TRUE or FALSE on their sheets. At the end, go back over them and give the group the right answers. Do not stop to ask who got them right!

1   MANDIBLE
(a) A victorian invention for squeezing the water out of wet washing. (FALSE)
(b) An insect's upper jaw or part of a bird's beak. (TRUE)

2   NOSTRUM
(a) A quack remedy, patent medicine. (TRUE)
(b) The raised platform on which the conductor of an orchestra stands. (FALSE)

3   TRIUMVIR
(a) The male member of the Royal Family who is third in line to the throne. (FALSE)
(b) Each member of a group of three men forming a united office or role. (TRUE)

4   BUSBY
(a) A yellow bird of South American origin. (FALSE)
(b) A tall fur cap worn by hussars and guardsmen. (TRUE)

5   OPHIDIAN
(a) A member of the reptile family Ophidia or Serpentes which includes snakes. (TRUE)
(b) A precious stone. (FALSE)

6   URIM
(a) An ancient form of thimble worn when making religious garments. (FALSE)
(b) Objects worn in or on the breastplate of a Jewish high priest. (TRUE)

7   WELCH
(a) The way the Royal Welch Fusiliers spell Welsh. (TRUE)
(b) A north-country word for wet mud. (FALSE)

Bible reading

This session is called, 'Pull the other one!' It is about doubt and we are going to take a look at an incident in the life of Thomas, one of Jesus' twelve disciples. The incident is recorded in **John 20:19–29**.

> Read the passage yourself or, if someone else has volunteered to do so, invite them to read it to the group now.

Discussion

1 We begin to doubt the truth of things we have been taught when we come across other factors which seem to contradict them or suggest that they may only be part of the truth. What we have believed as 'the truth' is called into question so gives rise to doubt.

What might have caused Thomas to doubt that Jesus had risen from the dead?

2 How far are our doubts purely intellectual? What other factors could make us prone to doubt Christian teaching or at least make it difficult to believe?

> It might be helpful to encourage the group to think about how some of the following affect our ability to believe the truth. Write them up on a flip-chart for everyone to see: personal circumstances; poor information; popular opinion; scientific information; ill health in general and emotional ill health in particular; personal insecurity; negative thinking; a narrow and dogmatic presentation of Christian truth; one's stage of growth and maturity, eg adolescence, mid-life, etc; possible Satanic influence.
>   Then ask:
> Which of these things might have affected Thomas and caused him to doubt?

3 Have you ever found yourself being confronted by doubt? What was it that you doubted, and how did you come to terms with your doubts?

In what ways have you found that doubt has actually *helped* you in your growth towards maturity as a Christian?

4 Let's look at the passage. How did Thomas deal with his doubts?

> There are two points the group could draw out:
> ● Thomas was prepared to face his uncertainty and acknowledge that he needed to resolve it.
> ● He brought it into the open, sharing it with his closest associates.

5 One of the things that often accompanies doubt is the feeling that God will not accept doubters. There is a strong feeling that God disapproves of doubters and will not bother to help such a person. What does this incident show us about the way God reacts to people with doubts?

6 Let's look up two other passages. For each we will ask:
(a) who was doubting?
(b) what might have caused it?
(c) how did God respond?

> Read out the following to the group, allowing time for discussion after each.

● 1 Kings 19:1–9
● Matthew 11:1–6

Action
What can we do in future to help others in the church cope with doubts?

Reading for next session

It would be helpful if each of us could read through the book of Ruth before the next session. Our discussion time will be based on this book. It only has four small chapters so it should not take too long. It's found between the book of Judges and 1 Samuel, starting on page . . .

Arrangements for the final session

It would be good to have an informal get-together after this series has finished, simply to round it off with some fun together. Some ideas are listed on pages 90–91. It might be helpful to discuss now what your group would like to do then, so that plenty of time can be given for making arrangements. Make sure that absent members are informed about the arrangements in good time so that they can come along. Group members might like to help in the informing process.

Prayer

Pray yourself or use the following prayer:

'Lord, help us to cope more constructively with the doubts that confront us. Help us to be more ready to listen to people's uncertainties and more able to help them get to the root of the problem. Help us together to grow in faith and reach a deeper maturity in Christ. Amen.'

Coffee and chat

Do not forget to fill in the register on page 96.

10

Out in the cold

Ruth

Preparation

This week you will need a large piece of paper. Again, the reverse side of a sheet of wallpaper will do. Write on this the four suggested causes of loneliness, printed in italics in question 1. All you need to write out are the headings lettered A, B, C and D. You also need to have prepared a large sheet listing the five points of 'The Boaz Method' (see 'Action' section). Have a spare sheet of paper ready to compile the group's own list of suggestions in response to question 4. You will also need a piece of paper and a pen for yourself.

For the 'Why not?' exercise you will need newspapers and magazines, a pair of scissors for each group member and a handy waste paper basket.

Welcome

Prayer

Pray yourself or use the following prayer:

'Thank you, Lord, for your presence with us

throughout the weeks we have spent together and for the love and understanding which has grown up between us. Help us to build on what we have learned from our discussions. Once more we ask that your presence among us will aid our understanding of your word and continue to deepen our relationships with one another. Amen.'

Report back

Once again, give group members a chance to report back on their experiences of using their gifts and abilities. As this is the last 'Report back' session it might be helpful if some of the time was spent discussing what each member is going to do in the weeks that lie ahead with regard to the remaining gifts and abilities on their list.

If your church is organizing a special service in which group members can offer their gifts and abilities, give details of the arrangements at this point.

If the group decided to take action after last week's discussion on 'Doubt' time should also be taken to report back on the results.

Why not?

Read the papers

Collect a variety of old newspapers and magazines from your friends. You will also need enough pairs of scissors for each person to have one. Pass round the scissors and ask the group members to attack the papers and magazines, cutting out any picture or headline which expresses 'loneliness'.

After five minutes ask each person in turn to hold up the pictures and headlines they found and to say briefly why they felt those pictures or headlines described 'loneliness'.

Clear away the rest of the newspapers before moving on to the Bible reading.

Bible reading

Today we are going to look at the problem of loneliness. The title for this session is, 'Out in the cold' and our character is Ruth. I hope you've been able to look through this little book; at this point let's just read **Ruth chapter 2** and then we'll refer to other verses as we go along.

Discussion

1 Which of the following possible causes of loneliness would you say is the most common cause of loneliness?

A *Loneliness as a state of mind*
(People who think they are lonely often create for themselves a lonely existence.)

B *Loneliness created by circumstances*
(Things happen that result in people unavoidably becoming lonely, such as bereavement, divorce, moving house.)

C *Loneliness caused by low self esteem*
(People who do not like themselves feel they are unlovable and become lonely as a result.)

D *Loneliness as a by-product of personality*
(Some people are loners; they choose to be alone and enjoy it.)

2 What two events led to Ruth's loneliness?

3 Let's make a list of the sort of people in our own neighbourhood who, like Ruth, may experience loneliness because of the circumstances they find themselves in.

Note down the group's suggestions for use later. If the following are not mentioned you could suggest them yourself: widows, divorcees, single people living alone, a mum at home with small children, college students away from home, children away at school (if appropriate), new arrivals in the area, a Christian in a non-Christian home, disabled people, those nursing sick or invalid members of the family. Make sure you allow the group enough time to come up with their own suggestions before raising these.

4 Boaz did five very constructive things for Ruth. What were they? See chapter 2 verses 5, 8, 14, 15–16, and chapter 3 verses 12–13.

A summary list is set out below. Write down the group's suggestions as they make them – either in their own words or as follows. Make sure the end product is large enough for everyone to see.
- 2:5   He noticed her
- 2:8   He talked to her
- 2:14   He tried to include her in the group
- 2:15–16 He showed her kindness
- 3:12–13 He took practical steps to help her

5 It is possible, because of changing circumstances, to forget what loneliness is like, though we may have experienced it. What *does* it feel like to be lonely? What lonely periods in your life can you recall, and what feelings went with them?

Allow enough time for people to contribute here before moving on. It will take some group members considerable courage to talk honestly about painful experiences.

Having given the group time to respond, use the next question to explore this aspect of loneliness further.

6 What did other people do to help you during those times of loneliness, which you might now be able to do for others? What would you like other people to do if you found yourself in that situation again?

Action

Let's take a look at the list we compiled of lonely people in our neighbourhood in answer to question 3.

● Which of the categories on our list do we have in our church? Let's note down the names of some of the people.

● Let's try to respond to these lonely people in the ways Boaz responded to Ruth. It may help if we try a similar method or take similar steps to Boaz.

Display the list entitled 'The Boaz Method' (see below) and refer the group back to the one they drew up in response to question 4. Use both to encourage the group to see what practical steps they can take towards helping the lonely people they have identified.

The Boaz Method
1 Take particular notice of lonely people
2 Talk to them
3 Try to include them in your circle of friends
4 Show them kindness
5 Take practical steps to help

Next session

If you discussed arrangements for the next session last week, make sure you confirm the final details now. Also make sure the absent members are informed and invited to come along. The suggested list of ideas for the informal session are set out on pages 90–91.

Prayer

You may find that individual group members may like to say short prayers giving thanks to God for something they have

As we close in prayer tonight one of two or you may like to say a short sentence-prayer of thanks to God for the things you and others have gained from these sessions. If you want to say a prayer, do so in the silence that follows and we will say 'Amen' after it.

'Let us pray.' (Silence.)
    'Lord, we thank you for all the things each of us has gained by sharing in these group meetings. May the things you have taught us live on in our memory and may they find their way out in our lives in ways that will bring you praise and honour. Amen.'
    Now let's say 'The grace' together and look at each other as we say the words.
    'The grace of our Lord Jesus Christ, and the love of God, and the fellowship of the Holy Spirit be with us all evermore. Amen.'

Coffee and chat

An informal get-together

To round off this series of house groups it is suggested that we hold a more informal get-together so that we can relax and enjoy one another's company in a totally different atmosphere. Which of the following suggestions do you warm to as a group?

- A barbecue; where we bring our own food and drinks.
- A meal out; maybe at a Steak House, Carvery or Pizza Hut.
- A fun and games evening; with light refreshments.
- A buffet or meal at someone's home; to which we all bring food, etc.
- An evening out; at a local theatre, for instance.
- An evening of our own making. If you have any alternative ideas we can spend an evening 'doing our own thing'.

Be sure to make firm, detailed arrangements now, as this will save you a lot of running around in the intervening period. And be sure to let absent members of the group know about the arrangements in good time so that they can come along if they wish to.

Suggestions
for
church leaders

Sermons

These house group notes can be used as the basis for a series of sermons that tie in with the midweek programme. The sermons can either introduce the subjects or follow them up after the midweek discussion and can be given the same titles as the sessions.

Special service for the offering of gifts and abilities

As a culmination of this series, a special service could be arranged, containing an act of dedication. Group members may be encouraged to offer their gifts and abilities, which have been highlighted during the gift-spotting exercise. This act of dedication could form a central part of the service. If stone-shaped cardboard cut-outs are used to record the individual's gifts and abilities, a collage can be created on a large sheet of paper, possibly on one of the walls in the church or on the floor. As those offering their gifts and abilities come forward, they attach their cardboard cut-out of a stone with their gifts and abilities listed on it, to the sheet of paper, so building a collage 'wall'. The cardboard cut-outs can be stuck on with *Blu Tak*. Explain to the congregation that this is a symbolic way for individuals to offer themselves and the gifts they possess to God for use in his service. Where real stones are used a space on the floor will need to be cleared – or a large table used – where the stones can be placed during this act of dedication.

The service can focus on the words of 1 Peter 2:4–5, where Peter speaks about members of the church coming to Christ like living stones and letting him build them into the living fabric of the church. 1 Peter 4:7–11 takes this concept further, encouraging individuals to put their spiritual gifts into active service.

Using the gifts and abilities offered
Ways must be found of taking up and using the gifts and abilities offered during this service. The ways in which people should be asked to use their gifts will, of course, depend on the sort of gifts and abilities offered.

The church leadership also needs to consider any findings or recommendations which the group makes to it over the course of these studies, and to decide what action should be taken.

Leading a training session
If you are leading a training session for house group leaders it may be helpful to split the training period into two sessions. Below are a number of suggestions for how to incorporate some group exercises,

based on the items listed on pages 8–25. Wherever possible list the points you are making on an OHP, blackboard or marker board and photocopy the cartoons onto OHP acetates. This will help people to concentrate on the points being made.

1 Aims of the group leader
After outlining the aims (page 11) allow a few moments for questions. Then ask the group to get into pairs and (with your list covered up) to recall all four aims from memory.

2 Introductions
Once you have completed the description of how to introduce group members (pages 12–14), ask people to get into the same pairs as before and to compile information about each other, as outlined. After four minutes ask the pairs to link up with one other pair and to introduce each other in the way set out in the notes – first introducing themselves and then their partner.

3 Use of the Bible
Encourage the group as a whole to discuss this section (pages 14–16) and then ask them to recall, in pairs, the five reasons for using the Bible in this way.

4 Discussion
After going over the points made in the training session, give the group a chance to ask questions or discuss particular points.

5 Handling shy or over-talkative members
After covering this point in the section on 'Discussion' (pages 17–20), ask the group to form sub-groups of three and to:
a) discuss how they would handle a shy member;
b) role play one of the suggested approaches to

handling an over-talkative member. One of the three will need to take the part of the group leader, one will be the talkative group member, and the third should listen with a view to giving some comment on how the 'group leader' came across.

6 *Prayer*
Allow time for the whole group to discuss the approach outlined on pages 22–23. Then ask them to recall, in pairs the three reasons given for taking this approach.

7 *Keeping a register*
Ask the group to look at the register on page 96, after you have spoken about it. Allow them time to discuss the value of this exercise and to suggest how the best use could be made of the register.

Register

Name	Address and phone number	1	2	3	4	5	6	7	8	9	10	11
	Total											